First World War
and Army of Occupation
War Diary
France, Belgium and Germany

2 DIVISION
2 Light Brigade
Royal Irish Rifles
12th Battalion
1 April 1919 - 31 October 1919

WO95/1374/8

The Naval & Military Press Ltd
www.nmarchive.com
Published in association with The National Archives

Published by

The Naval & Military Press Ltd

Unit 10 Ridgewood Industrial Park,

Uckfield, East Sussex,

TN22 5QE England

Tel: +44 (0) 1825 749494

www.naval-military-press.com

www.nmarchive.com

This diary has been reprinted in facsimile from the original. Any imperfections are inevitably reproduced and the quality may fall short of modern type and cartographic standards.

© **Crown Copyright**
Images reproduced by permission of The National Archives, London, England, 2015.

Contents

Document type	Place/Title	Date From	Date To
Heading	WO95/1374/8		
Heading	2 Division 2 Light Brigade 12 Bn R Irish Rifles 1919 Apr-1919 Oct From 108 Bde 36 Div Box 2506		
War Diary	Arnolds Weiler	01/04/1919	30/04/1919
War Diary	Stommeln	01/05/1919	17/06/1919
War Diary	Bickendorf	18/06/1919	28/06/1919
War Diary	Riehl Barracks	29/06/1919	01/07/1919
War Diary	Stommeln	02/07/1919	09/07/1919
War Diary	Haan	10/07/1919	31/07/1919
Miscellaneous	Honours and Awards for July 1919		
War Diary	Haan	01/08/1919	31/08/1919
War Diary	Haan Germany	01/10/1919	23/10/1919
War Diary	Opladen	24/10/1919	30/10/1919
War Diary	Germany	31/10/1919	31/10/1919

woas|13748

2 (~~LIGHT~~) DIVISION

2 LIGHT BRIGADE

12 BN. R. IRISH RIFLES

1919 APR — 1919 OCT

FROM 108 BDE 36 DIV

Box 2506

WAR DIARY

INTELLIGENCE SUMMARY

Army Form C. 2118.

(Erase heading not required.)

Instructions regarding War Diaries and Intelligence Summaries are contained in F.S. Regs., Part II. and the Staff Manual respectively. Title pages will be prepared in manuscript.

Place	Date	Hour	Summary of Events and Information	Remarks and references to Appendices
ARNOLDSWEILER	1/4/19.		Battalion Strength. 49 Off. 1.059 O.Rs.	
	1/4/19.		Battalion Bathing in DUREN. "A" and "B" Companies trained during forenoon.	
	2/4/19.	0915 hours.	Battalion Inspection. Companies Training as follows:- 1 hour Close Order Drill ½ hour Physical training, ½ hour Guard Drill, ½ hour Handling of Arms, and Company Drill for N.C.Os. ½ hour Lecture. Lewis Gun and Education Classes carried on.	
	3/4/19.		As for 2nd inst.	
	4/4/19.		As for 3rd inst.	
	5/4/19.		Commanding Officer's Inspection of billets, followed by inspection by Medical Officer.	
	6/4/19.		Church Parades.	
	7/4/19.		As for 4th inst.	
	8/4/19.	0600 hours.	Battalion entrained at DUREN station, and detrained at ROMMERSKIRCHEN, and marched to STOMMELN to Billets.	
	9/4/19.		As for 7th inst.	
	10/4/19.		As for 9th inst.	
	11/4/19.		Battalion Route March.	
	12/4/19.		Commanding Officer's inspection of billets, followed by inspection by Medical Officer.	
	13/4/19.		Church Parades.	
	14/4/19.		As for 10th inst.	
	15/4/19.		As for 14th inst.	
	16/4/19.		As for 15th inst.	
	17/4/19.		Battalion Route March.	
	18/4/19.		Church Services.	
	19/4/19.		Commanding Officer's inspection of billets followed by kit inspection, and Medical Officer's inspection.	
	20/4/19.		Church Services.	
	21/4/19.		Holiday.	
	22/4/19.		The G.O.C. 2nd Light Brigade, inspected the Battalion.	
	23/4/19.		Battalion Bathing.	
	24/4/19.		Battalion Route March.	

WAR DIARY
or
INTELLIGENCE SUMMARY.

(Erase heading not required.)

Army Form C. 2118.

Place	Date	Hour	Summary of Events and Information	Remarks and references to Appendices
	25/4/19.		(CONTINUED).	
		0900 Hours.	Battalion Inspection. Companies training as follows:- One Company on Range and Musketry. Three Companies, Close Order Drill, Arm Drill, Ceremonial, and Physical training. N.C.Os, Signallers, Lewis Gun, and Buglers Classes.	
	26/4/19.		Commanding Officer's inspection of billets, followed by kit inspection, and Medical Officer's inspection.	
	27/4/19.		Church Parades.	
	28/4/19.		As for 25th inst.	
	29/4/19.		As for 28th inst.	
	30/4/19.		As for 29th inst.	

John Gallagher

F. Lieut-Col.,
Commanding,
12th (S) Battn. The Royal Irish Rifles.

Honours and Awards for April, 1919.

Capt. I. S. Duncan, M. C.   Chevalier de L'Ordre de La Couronne, and Croix de Guerre.

4th May, 1919.

12th (S) BATTN.
ROYAL IRISH
RIFLES.

Army Form C. 2118.

WAR DIARY
or
INTELLIGENCE SUMMARY

(Erase heading not required.)

Instructions regarding War Diaries and Intelligence Summaries are contained in F. S. Regs., Part II. and the Staff Manual respectively. Title pages will be prepared in manuscript.

Place	Date	Hour	Summary of Events and Information	Remarks and references to Appendices
	1919.			
SOMMELN.	May 1st/2nd.		Inspection of Battalion by Brigadier-General. 0900 Hours. Morning Inspection by the Commanding Officer. "D" Company on Range for Musketry. "A" "B" and "C" Companies. - ½ Hour Close Order Drill and handling of arms. ½ Hour Guard Duties. ½ Hour saluting with and without arms. ½ Hour Physical Training. 1 Hour Lewis Gun Training and Musketry.	
"	3rd.		Inspection of Billets by the Commanding Officer, followed by Medical Officer's Inspection. Church Services.	
"	4th.		Battalion Inspection at 0900 Hours. "A" and "B" Companies proceeded to COLOGNE for trip up the Rhine. "C" and "D" Companies at the disposal of Company Commanders.	
"	5th.		Training as for the 2nd inst.	
"	6th.		Inspection of Battalion by the Divisional General.	
"	7th.		Training as for the 2nd inst.	
"	8th.		Training as for the 8th inst.	
"	9th.		Inspection of billets by the Company Commanders, followed by Medical Officer's inspection.	
"	10th.		Church Services.	
"	11th.		Inspection Parade. "D" Company on Range for Musketry. "A" Company march to Brigade Training Area for extended order drill. Musketry fire orders. Physical Training. "B" and "C" Companies. ½ Hour close order drill and handling or arms. ½ Hour Guard duties and saluting with and without arms. ½ Hour Musketry and Bombing and ½ Hour Physical Training for Rifle sections only. 1 Hour Lewis Gun training for Lewis Gun Sections. 1 Hour Education Compulsory and voluntary. Military training for those not on Education.	
"	12th.		Companies at the disposal of Company Commanders for Ceremonial Drill.	
"	13th.		Training as for the 13th.	
"	14th.		Rehearsal for Commander-in-Chief's inspection at GILL.	
"	15th.		Companies at the disposal of Company Commanders.	
"	16th.		Inspection by the Commander-in-Chief at GILL.	
"	17th.		Church Services.	
"	18th.			

Army Form C. 2118.

WAR DIARY
or
INTELLIGENCE SUMMARY
(Erase heading not required.)

Instructions regarding War Diaries and Intelligence Summaries are contained in F. S. Regs., Part II. and the Staff Manual respectively. Title pages will be prepared in manuscript.

Place	Date		Hour	Summary of Events and Information	Remarks and references to Appendices
1919					
STOMMELN.	May	19th.		As for the 18th for "A" "B" and "D" Companies. "C" Company working on Brigade Range.	
"	"	20th.		Training as for the 19th for "B" "C" and "D" Companies. "A" Company as for "C" on the 19th.	
"	"	21st.		Route March for all Companies.	
"	"	22nd.		Training for "B" and "C" Companies as for "A" and "D" on 21st. training for "A" and "D" Companies as for "B" and "C" on the 21st.	
"	"	23rd.		0800 Hours. "A" and "D" Companies on Range. 0900 Hours "B" and "C" Companies morning inspection & training as for the 21st inst. Cricket v-8th Bn/Welch V 4th Fusils R.E. Battalion beat	
"	"	24th.		Headquarters Company on Range for Musketry. Billet inspection by Company Commanders followed by Medical Officers inspection.	
"	"	25th.		Church Services.	
"	"	26th.		Training as for the 23rd inst.	
"	"	27th.		Training as for the 26th inst.	
"	"	28th.		Training as for the 27th inst.	
"	"	29th.		Battalion Route March.	
"	"	30th.		Training as for the 28th inst.	
"	"	31st.		Billet inspection by the Commanding Officer, followed by Medical Officer's inspection. Headquarters Company on Range for Musketry. Brigade Cricket Cup Competition. Brigade Headquarters v 12th Royal Irish Rifles. The Battalion won by 130 runs.	
	3rd June 1919.				

L. Lieut-Col.
Commanding.
12th (S) Battn. The Royal Irish Rifles.

12th (S) BATTN.
ROYAL IRISH
RIFLES.

WAR DIARY or INTELLIGENCE SUMMARY

Army Form C. 2118.

Place	Date	Hour	Summary of Events and Information	Remarks and references to Appendices
STOMMELN. 1919.				
	June 1st.		Church Parades.	
	2nd.		Inspection parade. "A" and "B" Companies on range for qualifying Musketry Course. "C" Company march to Brigade Training Area, GILL, , under O.C. Company for Extended Order drill, Musketry fire orders, Physical Training etc. "D" Company ¾ hour Close Order drill and handling arms, ¼ hour Guard duties and saluting with and without arms, ½ hour Musketry, bombing, and physical training (for rifle sections only). 1 hour Lewis Gun training, for Lewis Gun sections, 1 hour Education - compulsory and voluntary. - Military training for those not attending Education.	
	3rd.		Special Battalion parade at 1000 hours when all Guards turn out and give a Royal Salute, to Lieut-Col. W.R.Goodwin, C.M.G., D.S.O., assumed temporary command of the 2nd Light Brigade. celebrate aniversary of birthday of His Majesty the King. Remainder of the day observed as a holiday.	
	4th.		Inspection parade. "C" and "D" Companies on range for qualifying Musketry Course. "A" Company as for "C" Company for 2nd inst., "B" Company as for "D" Company for 2nd.	
	5th.		Battalion route march, accompanied by 1st Line Transport.	
	6th.		Inspection parade. "A" and "B" Companies on range for qualifying Musketry Course. "A" Company as for "C" Company for 2nd inst. "C" Company as for "D" Company for 2nd inst.	
	7th.		Billet inspection under Company arrangements. Medical inspection of Companies by Medical Officer. Cricket match between Battalion and C/190 R.F.A. Battalion beaten by 3 runs.	
	8th.		Church Parades.	
	9th.		General holiday, being Whit Monday. Inter-Company Cricket Matches.	
	10th.		Inspection parade. "C" and "D" Companies on range. "A" and "B" Companies march to Brigade Training Area under Company Commanders for Platoon training as per S.S. 143. Education - Battalion Test Examination at 1350 hours.	
	11th.		"A" and "B" Companies as for 10th inst. "C" Company parade on Battalion parade ground for platoon training. "D" Company and "H.Q." Company on range for musketry.	
	12th.		Battalion route march accompanied by 1st Line Transport.	
	13th.		Inspection parade. "A" and "B" Companies as for 10th inst. "D" Company on Battalion parade ground for platoon training. "C" Company and "H.Q." Company on range for musketry.	
	14th.		Inspection of billets by the Commanding Officer, followed by Medical inspection and short lecture to all ranks by Medical Officer. Kit inspection under Company arrangements.	

Army Form C. 2118.

WAR DIARY
or
INTELLIGENCE SUMMARY.
(Erase heading not required.)

Instructions regarding War Diaries and Intelligence Summaries are contained in F. S. Regs., Part II. and the Staff Manual respectively. Title pages will be prepared in manuscript.

Place	Date	Hour	Summary of Events and Information	Remarks and references to Appendices
1919.				
STOMMELN.	June 14th.		(CONTINUED). Cricket Match V 9th London Regiment. Battalion won.	
	June 15th.		Church Parades. Cricket match.	
	16th.		Inspection Parade. "A" and "B" Companies on range for Musketry. "C" and "D" Companies march to Brigade Training Area under Company Commanders for platoon training as per S.S. 143.	
	17th.		Lecture by Mr. E.G. Howell on "The Balkan Tangle". Orders having been received to move forward, "A", "B", and "D" Companies left by Bus for COLOGNE, to relieve the city guards found by the Northern Division, spending the night in RIEHL BARRACKS.	
BICKENDORF.	18th.		Battalion, less "A", "B", and "D" Companies moved in accordance with Operation Orders, staging at BICKENDORF. "A", "B", and "D" Companies mounted guards in City of COLOGNE and MULHEIM BRIDGE, relieving guards found by the 3rd Brigade, Northern Division.	
	19th.		Battalion, less "A", "B", and "D" Companies, proceeded by march route to Infantry Barracks, RIEHL, and took over quarters from 20th Battn. Durham Light Infantry.	
	20th.		Inspection of barrack rooms by the Commanding Officer. Cleaning up Barracks, and fitting of equipment.	
	21st.		Inspection of barrack rooms and billets by the Commanding Officer, followed by Medical inspection and short lecture to Companies by the Medical Officer. Kit inspection under Company arrangements. Lieut-Col. W. R. Goodwin, C.M.G., D.S.O., resumed command of the Battalion.	
	22nd.		Church parades. Inspection of Barracks by Brigadier-General Commanding. Inspection of guards by the General Officer Commanding, Light Division.	
	23rd.		Cleaning up Barracks. "C" Company and "H.Q." Company parade under Company arrangements. Inspection of guards by Brigadier-General Commanding 2nd Light Brigade.	
	24th.		Parades as for 23rd. Inspection of Barracks by Corps Commander.	
	25th.		Parades as for 23rd. G. O. C., Light Division visited and inspected Barracks.	
	26th.		Parades as for 25th.	
	27th.		Parades as for 25th.	
	28th.		Inspection of barrack rooms and billets by the Commanding Officer, followed by Medical inspection of Companies. Official information of Peace Treaty being signed announced by firing of 101 guns in COLOGNE.	

WAR DIARY
or
INTELLIGENCE SUMMARY.
(Erase heading not required.)

Army Form C. 2118.

Place	Date	Hour	Summary of Events and Information	Remarks and references to Appendices
1919.				
RIEHL BARRACKS.			(CONTINUED).	
	June 29th.		Church Parades.	
	30th.		All guards found by the Battalion in COLOGNE City and on MULHEIM BRIDGE relieved by the 52nd Durham Light Infantry.	
			[signature]	
			Major,	
			Commanding,	
			12th-(S) Battn. The Royal Irish Rifles.	
	4th July, 1919.		Honours and Awards for June, 1919.	
			Lieut-Col.W.R.Goodwin, D.S.O. C.M.G.	
			Lieut.A.M.Anderson, M.C.	
			15/12741. Sgt.Davidson.W. D.C.M.	
			12/18008. Col.Sgt.Kelly. C.D. M.S.M.	

12th (S) BATTN.
ROYAL IRISH
RIFLES.

No. 19389
Date 5/7/19

Army Form C. 2118.

WAR DIARY
or
INTELLIGENCE SUMMARY.
(Erase heading not required.)

Instructions regarding War Diaries and Intelligence Summaries are contained in F.S. Regs., Part II. and the Staff Manual respectively. Title pages will be prepared in manuscript.

Place	Date	Hour	Summary of Events and Information	Remarks and references to Appendices
	1919.			
RIEHL BARRACKS.	July. 1st.		Battalion proceeded by Lorries, in accordance with Operation Orders, to former billets in STOMMELN.	
STOMMELN.	2nd.		Inspection Parade. Companies at disposal of Company Commanders for cleaning billets, fitting of equipment, and Kit inspection. Lecture by Medical Officer.	
	3rd.		Inspection Parade. Companies at disposal of Company Commanders for re-organisation, etc. Education Classes.	
	4th.		Inspection Parade. "A" and "B" Companies on range, firing Musketry Course. "C" and "D" Companies march to Brigade Training Ground for Platoon Training as laid down in S.S.143. P.T. Class for Officers and N.C.O's.	
	5th.		Inspection of billets by the Commanding Officer. Medical Inspection and short lecture to all ranks by the Medical Officer. Kit inspection under Company arrangements. Examination for all men not yet passed Battalion Test Examination.	
	6th.		Church Parades.	
	7th.		Inspection Parade. Companies at disposal of Company Commanders for cleaning up etc.	
	8th.		Battalion Sports. Brigadier-General Commanding present during afternoon. Orders received for the Battalion to move tomorrow and relieve 11th Royal Scots in Outpost Line, and take over billets in HAAN. "C" Company in Outpost Line.	
	9th.		Battalion entrained at HOMMERSKIRCHEN, detrained at OHLIGS, and moved by March Route to HAAN. "C" Company took over Outpost Line.	
HAAN.	10th.		Companies at disposal of Company Commanders for cleaning up and re-fitting.	
	11th.		Companies at disposal of Company Commanders for Training. Physical Training and Education Classes.	
	12th.		Inspection of billets by Commanding Officer. Medical Inspection and Short Lecture by Medical Officer. Kit inspection under Company arrangements.	
	13th.		Church Parades. "D" Company relieved "C" Company in Outpost Line.	
	14th.		Inspection Parade. Companies at disposal of Company Commanders. "A" and "C" Companies for platoon training on Brigade Training Ground. "B" Company - Battalion duties - Musketry Course. Lewis Guns Sections under Lewis Gun Officer on Range. Agricultural Class under Lieut. A.M. Anderson, M.G. Education Classes.	

WAR DIARY
or
INTELLIGENCE SUMMARY.
(Erase heading not required.)

Army Form C. 2118.

Place	Date	Hour	Summary of Events and Information	Remarks and references to Appendices
HAAN. (CONTINUED).	July 15th.		Inspection Parade. "A" and "C" Companies for training as on 14th. "B" Company firing on Rifle Range at BRUCKERKOTEN. Education Classes.	
	16th.		Inspection Parade. Training and Education Classes as for the 14th.	
	17th.		Inspection Parade. Training and Education Classes as for 15th.	
	18th.		Battalion Route March. Educational Classes.	
	19th.		Inspection of Billets by the Commanding Officer. Medical Inspection and Lecture to Companies by the Medical Officer. Kit inspection, and fitting of Equipment. GENERAL HOLIDAY.	
	20th.		Church Parades.	
	21st.		Inspection Parades. "B" and "C" Companies, march to Brigade Training Area for Platoon Training as per S.S. 143. "A" Company - Battalion duties, firing Musketry Course, Lewis Gun Sections firing under Lewis Gun Officer on BRUCKERKOTEN RANGE. Education Classes.	
	22nd.		Rhine Trip.	
	23rd.		Peace Celebrations. Battalion Sports.	
	24th.		Route March, accompanied by First Line Transport. Education Classes.	
	25th.		Inspection parade. "A", "B", and "C" Companies under Company Commanders as for 21st.	
	26th.		Physical Training and Education Classes. Medical Inspection, and lecture by the Inspection of Billets by the Commanding Officer. Medical, Agricultural, and P. T. Classes.	
	27th.		Medical Officer. Kit inspection. Education, Agricultural.	
			Church Parades. "A" Company relieved "D" Company in Outpost Line.	
	28th.		Inspection Parade. "A" "C" and "D" Companies on Brigade Training Ground for Platoon Training as per S.S.143. "B" Company - Battalion duties, Platoon Training on Battalion Parade Ground. "D" Company refitting, clothing, equipment, etc., and bathing.	
	29th.		Battalion Route March.	
	30th.		Inspection Parade. "B", "C", and "D" Companies under Company Commanders as for 28th. Battalion Test Examination. Lecture on War Savings.	
	31st.		Inspection parade. "B", "C", and "D" Companies under Company Commanders as for 30th. P. T., Education, and Agricultural Classes.	

signature Lieut-Col.,
Commanding
12th (S)Battn. The Royal Irish Rifles.

Army Form C. 2118.

WAR DIARY
or
INTELLIGENCE-SUMMARY.
(Erase heading not required.)

Place	Date	Hour	Summary of Events and Information	Remarks and references to Appendices
			Honours and awards for July, 1919.	
			Mentioned in Sir Douglas Haig's Despatch of 16th March, 1919.	
			Lieut-Col. W.R.Goodwin, CMG, DSO.	
			Lieut. G.S. Doyle. 19140. Sgt. Bushe, J.H.	
			Capt. G.C. Hume. 40202. L/C. Atcheson, A.	
			Major E.R.H. May, DSO. 4863. Sgt. Magee, S.	
			Lieut. C.N. McCaull. 655. Cpl. McAuley, J.	
			Capt. G.N.L. Strong, MC. 16/48. Cpl. Potter, J.	
			19182. Sgt. Ramsey, J.	

12th (S) BATTN.
ROYAL IRISH RIFLES.
No. 2/533
Date 5/8/19

WAR DIARY
INTELLIGENCE SUMMARY

(Erase heading not required.)

Army Form C. 2118.

12 R1R

Place	Date	Hour	Summary of Events and Information	Remarks and references to Appendices
1919.				
HAAN.	Aug. 1st.		Inspection Parade. "A" Company finding Outpost Duties. "C" and "D" Companies under Company Commanders, march to Brigade Training Area for Platoon Training as per S.S. 143. "B" Company finding duties, remainder of Company, platoon training on Battalion parade Ground. Educational and Recreational Classes. Battalion Transport Show and Competition. Brigadier-General Commanding and Staff visited show during the afternoon.	
	2nd.		Inspection of billets by the Commanding Officer. Medical Inspection and short lecture to all ranks by the Medical Officer. Kit inspection under Company arrangements. Educational agricultural, P.T., and Lewis Gun Classes as usual. Inter-Company Basket Ball matches.	
	3rd.		Church Parades.	
	4th.		Battalion Holiday. Eliminating contests took place in connection with Battalion Sports being held on the 7th.	
	5th.		Inspection parade. "B" and "C" Companies on Brigade Training Ground for Company training. "D" Company finding duties - remainder of Company platoon training. Classes as usual.	
	6th.		as for the 5th. Battalion played thr 483rd Field Company R.E. at Cricket. Result:- 483rd Field Company won. Open-air Bathing.	
	7th.		Battalion Holiday. Sports held on Battalion Sports Ground. Band of 6th London Regiment attended. Brigadier-General Commanding and Staff visited during the afternoon. Concert in the evening.	
	8th.		Inspection parade. "B" and "C" Companies Route March. "D" Company platoon training. Educational and P.T. Classes.	
	9th.		Inspection of billets by the Commanding Officer. Medical Inspection and short lecture to all ranks by the Medical Officer. Kit inspection and fitting of equipment. Examination for 3rd Class Army Certificate held.	
	10th.		Church Parades. Company of 6th London Regiment relieved "A" Company in Outpost Line.	
	11th.		"B", "C", and "D" Companies on Brigade Training Ground for Company Training. "A" Company finding Battalion duties, remainder of Company platoon training on Battalion Parade Ground. Educational and other classes as usual. Open-air Bathing.	
	12th.		Inspection Parade. Route March by Companies, with Transport. Educational Classes. Battalion Cross-Country Run.	
	13th.		Inspection Parade. Companies at disposal of Company Commanders for Close Order, Handling Arms, and Ceremonial Drill. "D" Company Medical Inspection. Educational and Agricultural Class.	

Army Form C. 2118.

WAR DIARY
or
INTELLIGENCE SUMMARY.
(Erase heading not required.)

Instructions regarding War Diaries and Intelligence Summaries are contained in F. S. Regs., Part II. and the Staff Manual respectively. Title pages will be prepared in manuscript.

Place	Date	Hour	Summary of Events and Information	Remarks and references to Appendices
HAAN.	(Cont'inued).			
	Aug. 13th.		Battalion Boxing Contests, attended by Brigadier-General Commanding and Staff. Brigadier General Commanding presented prizes.	
	14th.		Parades and classes as for 13th. Inter-Company Cricket matches.	
	15th.		General Holiday. Brigade Sports held at BAVERT. General Officer Commanding and Staff Light Division attended as Brigadier General Commanding and Staff. Mrs. Robertson, wife of the Staff Captain, 2nd Light Brigade, presented the prizes. Bands of the 6th and 9th London Regiments attended.	
	16th.		Inspection of billets by the Commanding Officer. Medical Inspection and lecture by the Medical Officer. Kit inspection under Company arrangements. Educational Classes.	
	17th.		Church Parades.	
	18th.		Inspection Parades. Companies at disposal of Company Commanders for cleaning up and preparing for inspection by Army Council on 19th. Brigade Boxing Competition held at HAAN. Brigadier General Commanding attended with Staff and presented Medals.	
	19th.		Battalion proceeded by Bus to LEVERKUSEN and formed Guard of Honour for Army Council. Inspection by Colonel of the Regiment,-Field Marshall Sir Henry Wilson, G.C.B., D.S.O., Chief of the General Staff.	
	20th.		General Holiday. Brigade Cross Country Run and Basket Ball Competition held at BAVERT. Cup presented by Brigadier General Commanding to Battalion for scoring highest points in the Brigade Competition, won by 12th Royal Irish Rifles, and presented to Lieut-Col. W.R.Goodwin, C.M.G., D.S.O., by the Brigadier-General.	
	21st.		Inspection Parade. "C" Company firing Musketry Course. "A" Company – Company training. "D" Company finding duties – remainder of Company platoon training. "B" Company took over Outpost Line from 6th London Regiment.	
	22nd.		Inspection Parade. Parades as for 21st.	
	23rd.		Inspection of billets by the Commanding Officer. Medical Inspection and lecture to all ranks by the Medical Officer. Kit inspection under Company arrangements.	
	24th.		Church Parades.	
	25th.		Inspection Parade. "C" Company firing Musketry Course. "D" Company – Company Training. "A" Company finding Battalion duties – remainder of Company platoon training. Educational Classes as usual.	

WAR DIARY
or
INTELLIGENCE SUMMARY.
(Erase heading not required.)

Army Form C. 2118.

Place	Date	Hour	Summary of Events and Information	Remarks and references to Appendices
HAAN.	(Continued).			
	Aug. 26th.		Parades and classes as for 25th.	
	27th.		Parades and classes as for 26th.	
	28th.		Inspection Parade. "D" Company firing Musketry Course. "C" Company - Company training and Medical Inspection. "A" Company fiadir duties - remainder of Company, platoon training.	
	29th.		Classes as usual except for "D" Company.	
	30th.		Parades and classes as for 28th.	
			Inspection Parade. "D" Company firing Musketry Course. "A", "G", and "HQ" Companies at disposal of Company Commanders for kit inspection, etc. Medical inspection and lecture to all ranks by Medical Officer.	
	31st.		Educational Classes as usual. Church Parades.	

[signature] Lieut-Col.,
Commanding,
12th (S) Battn. The Royal Irish Rifles.

12th (S) BATTN.
ROYAL IRISH
RIFLES.
5th September, 1919.

Army Form C. 2118.

WAR DIARY
or
INTELLIGENCE SUMMARY.

(Erase heading not required.)

Instructions regarding War Diaries and Intelligence Summaries are contained in F. S. Regs., Part II. and the Staff Manual respectively. Title pages will be prepared in manuscript.

Place	Date	Hour	Summary of Events and Information	Remarks and references to Appendices
HAAN Germany	1/10/19.		"A" Coy in Outpost Line. "B" Coy finding duties and individual training. Education as usual. B Coy. "D" Coy and Transport bathed and all blankets disinfected at WALD.	
	2/10/19.		As for 1st. "C" Coy bathed.	
	3/10/19.		Training as for 2nd. H. Coy for medical inspection.	
	4/10/19.		"A" and H. Coys at disposal of Company Commanders for fitting of equipment. Kit inspection etc. Commanding Officer's inspection of billets. Entertainment by Mr. A. Spencer, Elocutionist.	
	5/10/19.		Church Parades.	
	6/10/19.		"B" Coy in Outpost Line. "A" Coy individual training and duties. Education as usual.	
	7/10/19.		As for 6th. Baths for A and H. Coys.	
	8/10/19.		As for 7th. Baths for B Coy and M Stores and Transport.	
	9/10/19.		As for 8th.	
	10/10/19.		As for 9th.	
	11/10/19.		Kit inspection for A and H. Coys. C.O's inspection of billets. Concert given by Miss May Joseph's Party.	
	12/10/19.		Church Parades.	
	13/10/19.		Companies at disposal of Company Commanders for training. Battalion bathed at WALD and blankets and clothing disinfected.	
	14/10/19.		Training as for 13th.	

Army Form C. 2118.

WAR DIARY
or
INTELLIGENCE SUMMARY.

(Erase heading not required.)

Instructions regarding War Diaries and Intelligence Summaries are contained in F. S. Regs., Part II. and the Staff Manual respectively. Title pages will be prepared in manuscript.

Place	Date	Hour	Summary of Events and Information	Remarks and references to Appendices
HAAN Germany	15/10/19.		As for 14th	
	16/10/19.		As for 15th	
	17/10/19.		As for 16th	
	18/10/19.		Inspection of billets by C.O.	
	19/10/19.		Church Parades.	
	20/10/19.		A and H. Coys at disposal of Company Commanders. B Coy in Outpost line.	
	21/10/19.		A. B and H. Companies bathed.	
	22/10/19.		A and H. Companies at disposal of Company Commanders. B Coy relieved in outpost line by 15th A.A.M.C.	
	23/10/19.		The Battalion moved to OPLADEN	
OPLADEN.	24/10/19.		Companies at disposal of Company Commanders. Medical Inspection for Battalion.	
	25/10/19.		As for 24th.	
	26/10/19.		Church Parades.	
	27/10/19.		As for 25th. Education as usual.	
	28/10/19.		As for 27th.	
	29/10/19.		As for 28th. Battalion bathed.	

Army Form C. 2118.

WAR DIARY
or
INTELLIGENCE SUMMARY.
(Erase heading not required.)

Instructions regarding War Diaries and Intelligence Summaries are contained in F. S. Regs., Part II. and the Staff Manual respectively. Title pages will be prepared in manuscript.

Place	Date	Hour	Summary of Events and Information	Remarks and references to Appendices
OPLADEN Germany.	30/10/19.		As for 29th.	
	31/10/19.		As for 30th.	

[signature] Lieut-Col. Commanding 12th (S) Battn. The Royal Irish Rifles.

www.ingramcontent.com/pod-product-compliance
Lightning Source LLC
Chambersburg PA
CBHW081509160426
43193CB00014B/2628